When God Asks...

Imagine the ultimate guest comes to dinner
and asks you some simple questions . . .

When God asks . . .

By Richard Wilkins

Rutledge Hill Press®
Nashville, Tennessee
A Thomas Nelson Company

Published by Rutledge Hill Press, a Thomas Nelson Company, P.O. Box 141000, Nashville, Tennessee 37214.

Library of Congress Cataloging-in-Publication Data

Wilkins, Richard, 1961-
    When God asks / by Richard Wilkins.
        p. cm.
     ISBN 1-55853-849-6
     1. Christian life—Miscellanea. I. Title.
BV4501.2 .W5323 2001
248.4—dc21

                                        00-046007
                                          CIP

Printed in Mexico
1 2 3 4 5 6—04 03 02 01

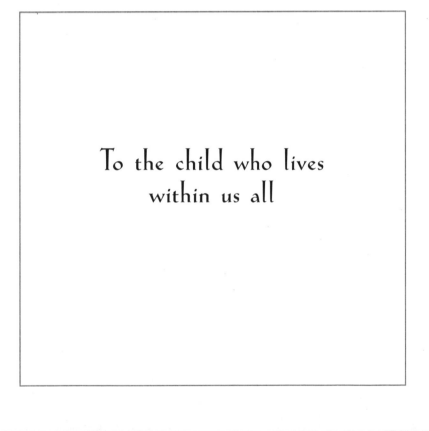

To the child who lives
within us all

Foreword

Please resist the temptation to simply
skip through these pages. Instead, stop
a while, and follow the wisdom
of your own answers.

Introduction

This book changed my life. It can change yours. It changed my life, not because I wrote it, but because I read it. I found that although my head was reading the questions, my heart was answering.

This book showed me how most of the time we are not living the life we really

mean to live, or being the person we
really mean to be.

Simply because we have forgotten, and
allowed our heads to deprive our hearts.

This book can show you where to improve
your life.

This book is a reminder of the life you
could be living, giving you the opportunity
to be the person you really mean to be; *ask
your heart*.

VIII

Imagine God, the ultimate guest, comes to dinner and begins asking you some simple questions about your life . . .

How do you see your future
if you don't change?

*D*o you complain about
the lack of flowers or do
you plant seeds?

Do you create happiness or do you chase after it?

Do you try to understand
as much as you want to
be understood?

*D*o you see through my
many disguises?

Do you love many people?

Do you encourage more
than you criticize?

Do you place as much
importance on how you think
as on how you look?

8

*D*o you give as much energy to your dreams as you do your fears?

9

Do you listen as much
as you talk?

Do you talk to strangers before they talk to you?

Do you see the good
in people as clearly as
you see their faults?

*D*o you make friends easily?

WHAT WILL YOU SAY?

$\mathcal{D}$o you notice when your prayers are answered?

WHAT WILL YOU SAY?

How often are you the first to say youre sorry?

Do you learn by others' mistakes or do you insist on struggling with your own?

Is it easy for you to share in the success of others?

*D*oes your honesty consider
the feelings of others?

Have you discovered the
difference between wanting
and needing?

Have you already
achieved goals you thought would
make you happy, but didn't?

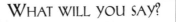

Do you leave much unsaid?

Are you aware that every reaction to every situation is a choice?

How does your pride
help you?

Is it important
for you to own?

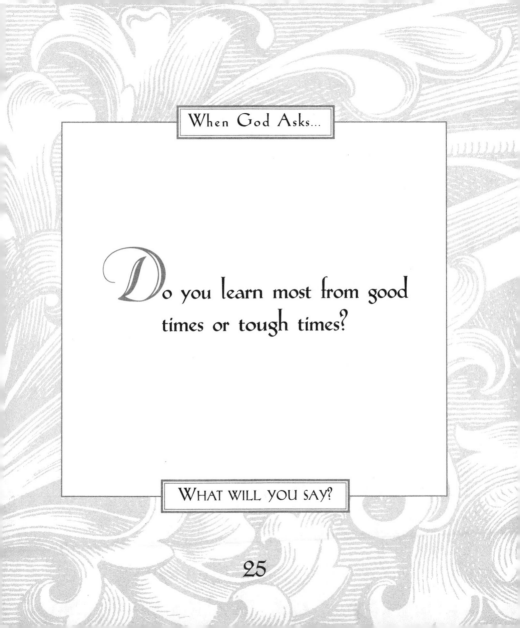

Do you learn most from good times or tough times?

Do you appreciate as much as
you take for granted?

Do you smile at people before they smile at you?

Do you spend much time exploring your potential?

28

Do you give much care to
what you put into your body?

Do you celebrate
the small things?

*D*o you search for wisdom?

WHAT WILL YOU SAY?

How often do you hold on
when you could let go?

$\mathcal{D}$o you review your options?

Do you dedicate much time
to children?

What will you be remembered for?

Do you want others' dreams
to come true?

*D*o you free yourself by
forgiving others?

What changes would you make if you could live your life again?

Do you take your life
too seriously?

Do you struggle before you
ask for help?

*D*o you walk far in
the shoes of others or do you
just try them on?

Do you value your friends as much as they deserve?

How long will you put off
living until you live life to the full?

$\mathcal{D}$o you pray as much to thank as to receive?

What stops you from being
more optimistic?

$\mathcal{I}$s your appreciation
too often too late?

How is worrying a problem
when you're not thinking about it?

WHAT WILL YOU SAY?

*D*o you pursue things you
know will hurt you?

48

Does your generosity match your desire for gain?

*D*oes feeling guilty help you?

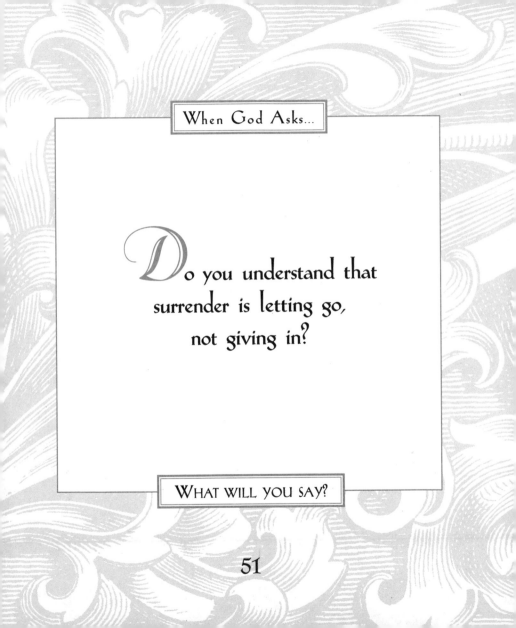

*D*o you understand that
surrender is letting go,
not giving in?

Why do you miss so much
that is beautiful?

When will you be satisfied?

Does your compassion move
you enough to take action?

*D*oes your tolerance equal the tolerance you expect from others?

Do you refuse to listen
to gossip?

*D*o you create opportunities
or wait for them?

Do you give up too easily?

*D*oes any possession
love you back?

What do you think
impresses me?

Which controls your life most, love or fear?

Are you fun to be with?

Do you appreciate the living
as much as you grieve the dead?

Do you ever doubt
my ability?

*D*o you blame your
circumstances or change them?

65

Do you do things you know
you will regret later?

$\mathcal{D}$o you make your
love conditional?

Do you dare to leap or do you need to be pushed?

Do you believe in miracles?

*D*o you acknowledge your achievements with the same ease you acknowledge your failures?

Do your fears live up
to your expectations of them?

71

*D*o you help keep your
planet healthy?

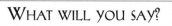

Do you sing your own song?

*D*oes your faith allow you
to accept what you don't
always understand?

Do you walk in the shadow of others or do you let your own light shine?

Do you resist change?

Does someone have to fall
before you help them?

Do you limit your dreams
by making them conditional
on becoming realities?

78

Would the world be a
better place if everyone followed
your example?

*D*o you leave your life to
chance by believing in luck?

Do you give your
life purpose?

Do you wish you
laughed more?

Could you give more
to charity?

Do you wish you took
more risks?

Do you think things go wrong just because they don't turn out the way you would like?

*D*o you judge people
by their appearance?

Do you know of anyone who
has found contentment in money?

Does the word 'change' mean fear or does it mean excitement for you?

Do you need a reason
to be happy?

*D*o you use the past as a
library or a home?

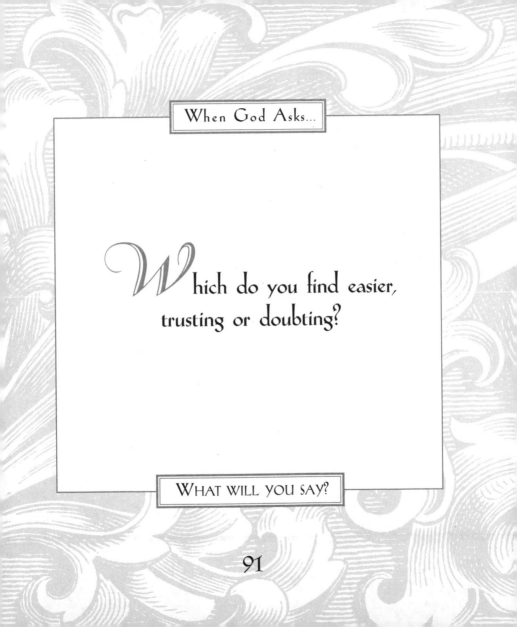

Which do you find easier,
trusting or doubting?

Would you like to think
better thoughts?

Who controls your thoughts?

Do you realize that
you can only keep hatred alive
in a memory?

Do you use the power of thought to improve your heart?

95

Do you wait for love
to come and knock on your door,
or do you go out and find it in
everything you can?

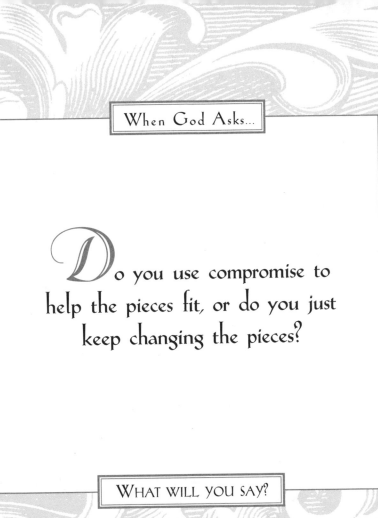

*D*o you use compromise to help the pieces fit, or do you just keep changing the pieces?

Do you like yourself as much
as you want others to like you?

$\mathcal{D}$o your mistakes become
lessons or guilt?

*D*o you see challenge
as struggle?

*D*o you put enjoyment into situations or expect to get it out of them?

Have you noticed how the priorities of dying people change?

*D*o you see your life
as an adventure?

Which is more important
to you; making a living or
making a difference?

Have you found security within yourself or are you still searching elsewhere?

How often do you
sing out loud?

Will you die without really living?

*W*hich is your greatest
motivation for change,
pain or pleasure?

Are you able to see a
competitor as a potential ally?

Do you fear the darkness or use it as an opportunity to shine?

Do you learn from children?

$\mathcal{A}$re you ever without hope?

*I*s your kindness obvious?

Who would impress you most, someone who had great wealth or someone who had real contentment?

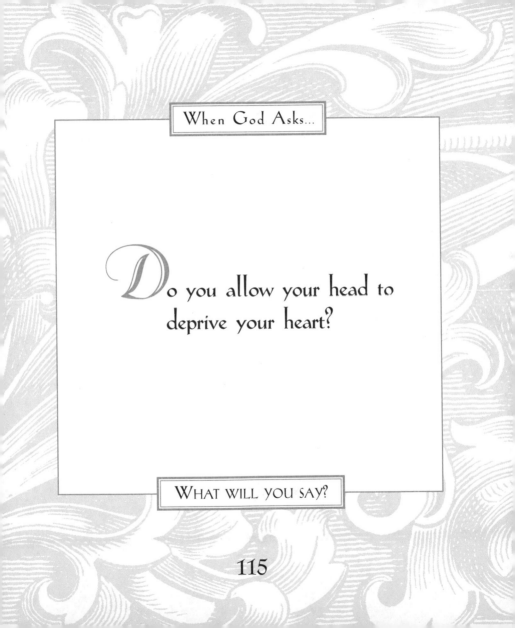

*D*o you allow your head to deprive your heart?

*D*o you need to touch to feel?

Can you see order in chaos?

Could you be more passionate
about your life?

*D*o you record the
special moments?

*W*ho creates your image
of yourself, you or the opinions
of others?

*D*o you act on the
priorities you voice?

*D*o you see children
as your equal?

*D*o you respect those who
have less than you?

Do you extend your kindness
to the unkind?

Have you discovered
that appreciation is the brightness
control on your life?

Do you greet the day
with gratitude?

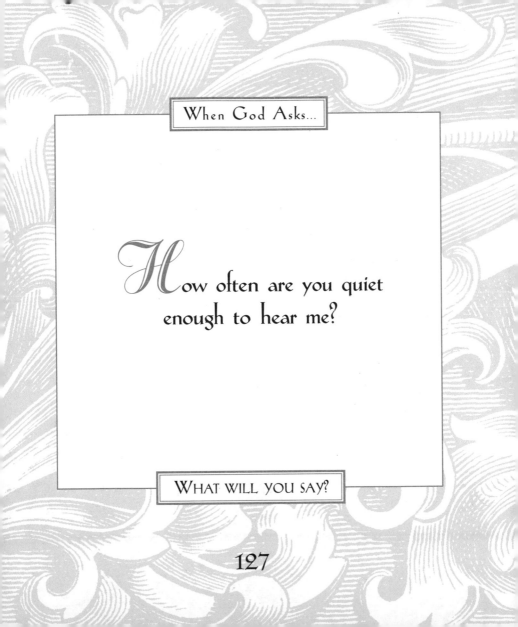

How often are you quiet
enough to hear me?

WHAT WILL YOU SAY?

Do you realize only you can label someone your enemy?

*D*o you use your imagination
to inspire your life?

*H*ave you retained the ability
to look with wonderment?

130

Can you see courage
in humility?

WHAT WILL YOU SAY?

What question would you like to ask me?

D̲o you accept what you cannot change?

Do you class yourself
a failure even when you have
given your best?

Do you accept age
with grace?

*H*ave you made a list
of the things you don't want and
don't have, to discover how much
you really have?

Do you observe without judgment?

*D*o you lend what
you could give?

Could more of your time be in service to others?

Do you judge or do you try
to understand?

Do you hold grudges?

When you make a mistake, which helps the most, understanding or punishment?

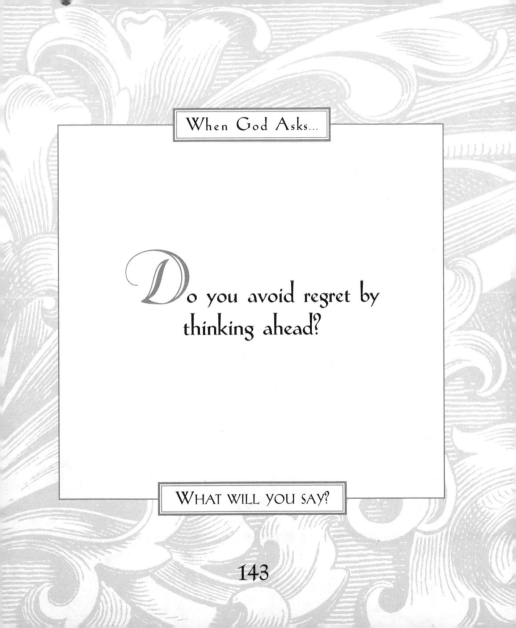

Do you avoid regret by
thinking ahead?

WHAT WILL YOU SAY?

143

Do you need a reason to send
a card or flowers?

Do you receive many
thank you cards?

Have your answers to these questions given you insight to your life?

Do you know how much
I love you?

*S*pecial thanks to the following for believing
in & sponsoring the printing of this book.
I hope when God asks them what they did to
help others they will remember to say: "I helped
make *When God Asks* available to the world".

Mark & Eileen Carr

Carol Abbott

Charles & Laurice Barnescone

Julian Baker & Louise Atwill

Tony & Gill Wilson

About the Author

Richard had never prayed so hard. The recession had struck, virtually overnight he crashed from being a self-made mutimillionaire to being broke, alone, and terrified on Rock Bottom.

In order to retain some sanity, Richard began writing down his thoughts and feelings. Applying the wisdom from this excercise changed his life, and his first book was born. Today, the same words that gave Richard a new lease on life are inspiring people around the world.